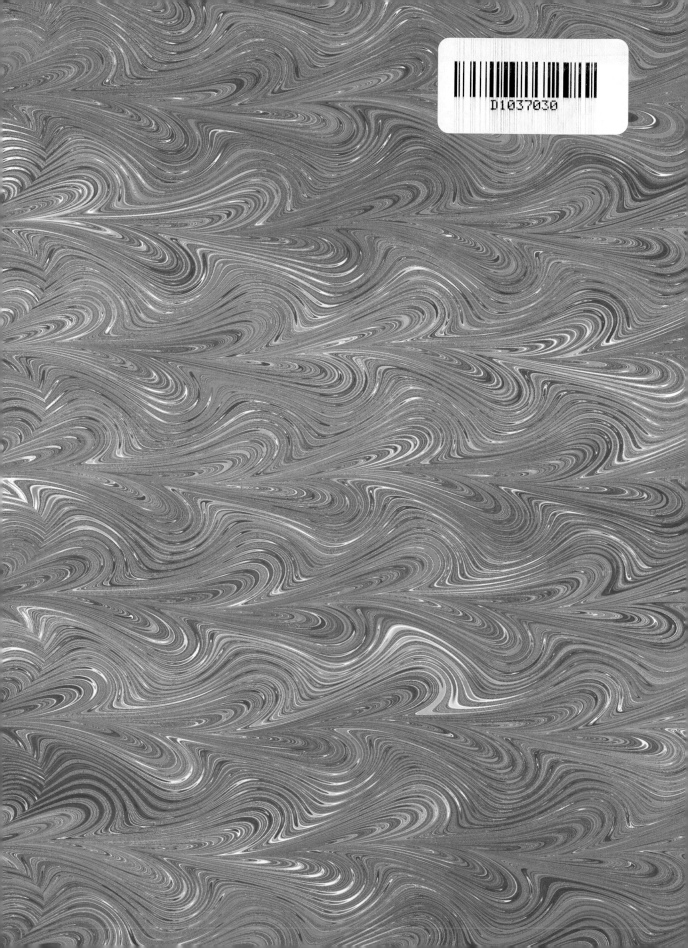

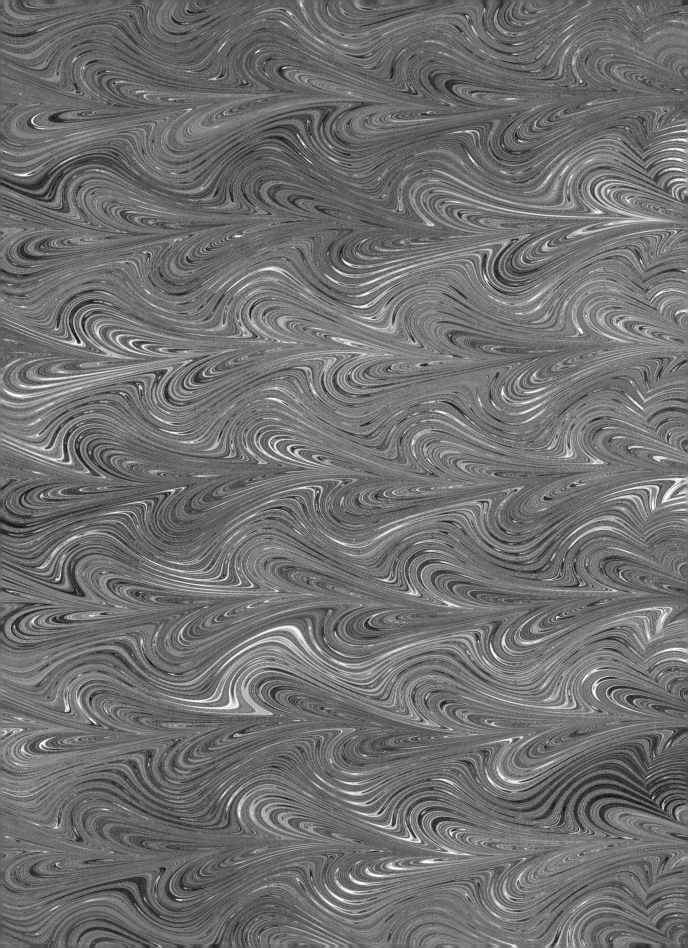

HISTORY
★ V·I·P ★

KING JOHN

BRILLIANT
BIOGRAPHIES
of the
DEAD FAMOUS

Paul Harrison

First published in Great Britain in 2015 by Wayland

Copyright © Wayland 2015

All rights reserved.

Editor: Annabel Stones

Illustration: Emmanuel Cerisier, Beehive Illustration

Designer: Rocket Design (East Anglia) Ltd

Proofreader: Rebecca Clunes

Consultant: Professor Nicholas Vincent, School of History, University of East Anglia

Dewey number: 942'.033'092-dc23

ISBN: 978 0 7502 8851 4

Library ebook ISBN: 978 0 7502 8856 9

10 9 8 7 6 5 4 3 2 1

Wayland

An imprint of Hachette Children's Group

Part of Hodder & Stoughton

Carmelite House

50 Victoria Embankment

London EC4Y 0DZ

An Hachette UK Company

www.hachette.co.uk

www.hachettechildrens.co.uk

Printed in China

Picture credits: Corbis Images: p.17 top © Heritage Images, p.20 © Bettmann, p.27 bottom © FACUNDO ARRIZABALAGA/epa; Mary Evans Picture Library: p.9; Shutterstock: p.7 Evgeny Shmulev, p.10 jorisvo, p.11 Georgios Kollidas, p.12 Tutti Frutti, p.17 bottom Panaiotidi, p.21 S.Borisov, p.23 Georgios Kollidas, p.25 Dave Head, p.27 top mstfcn, p.29 Roy Pedersen; Stefan Chabluk: p.4; Wikimedia Commons; p.22 CC Linda Spashett Storye book. All graphic elements: Shutterstock.

CONTENTS

page

Introducing
KING JOHN

King John ruled during a time of great upheaval and war. People know him as the king who was forced to sign something called Magna Carta. He was also the evil tyrant that Robin Hood fought, or so people will tell you. But was this really the full story of John's reign? Or has his reputation been smeared by history and actually he wasn't the monster he was said to be?

★ Bonjour England ★

The Plantagenet lands, also known as the Angevin Empire, reached their greatest extent under Henry II, John's father. They stretched from the Scottish borders to the south of France.

John was king during a time known as the Middle Ages or the medieval period. It was a difficult time to be alive as there were great wars, plagues and famine. However there were also great leaps forward in understanding and knowledge. Writing became more common and improvements were made in mathematics and medicine.

It was also a difficult time to be a ruler. John's kingdom was under constant threat from neighbouring kingdoms. He wasn't safe at home either as a number of his own barons wanted him replaced as king. John even managed to fall out with the head of the Catholic Church, the Pope. This was bad news during the Middle Ages as the Pope was one of the most powerful men in the world. However the question remains; how much of this was his own fault?

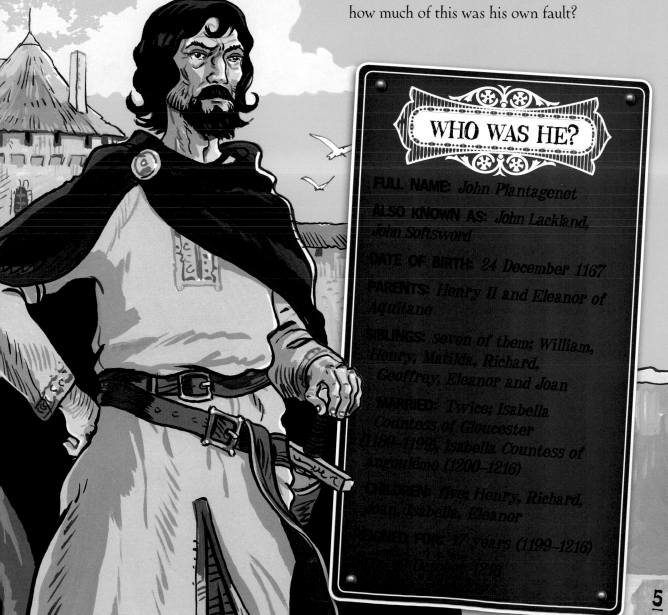

WHO WAS HE?

FULL NAME: John Plantagenet

ALSO KNOWN AS: John Lackland, John Softsword

DATE OF BIRTH: 24 December 1167

PARENTS: Henry II and Eleanor of Aquitane

SIBLINGS: seven of them; William, Henry, Matilda, Richard, Geoffrey, Eleanor and Joan

MARRIED: Twice; Isabella Countess of Gloucester (1189–1199), Isabella Countess of Angoulême (1200–1216)

CHILDREN: five; Henry, Richard, Joan, Isabella, Eleanor

REIGNED FOR: 17 years (1199–1216)

JOHN LACKLAND

John was the youngest child of King Henry II and Eleanor of Aquitaine. Unfortunately for John, his father had already given away much of his land to John's older siblings and there wasn't much left to pass on to John. He was nicknamed 'Lackland' as his father lacked any more land to give him!

Henry II was well known for having a terrible temper and according to reports from the time, so did John. In addition to his temper, John had a cruel streak and enjoyed making fun of people. However writers from the time also said he was intelligent and could often be generous when the fancy took him.

HENRY II

WILLIAM   HENRY   MATILDA

TRUE or FALSE?

JOHN'S GREAT-GRANDFATHER'S BODY EXPLODED.

true John was a direct descendent of William the Conqueror. When William died his body became so bloated it exploded when they tried to force it into his coffin.

Details of John's childhood are scarce but we do know that as the youngest son – and with no lands to call his own – it was decided that he should join the Church. Soon after his birth he was sent to the abbey at Fontevraud, in the Anjou region of France, with the aim of eventually becoming a bishop. For unknown reasons this didn't work out and instead he was educated by Ranulf de Glanvill, one of the King's closest advisors.

We also know that John spent little time with his parents, but this was normal for noble families. It was considered a good idea to educate the children of nobles away from their parents. At least John had an education – most children growing up in the Middle Ages never knew how to read or write and were expected to work at the earliest opportunity.

Fontevraud Abbey

ELEANOR OF AQUITAINE

KING RICHARD I

GEOFFREY

ELEANOR

JOAN

KING JOHN

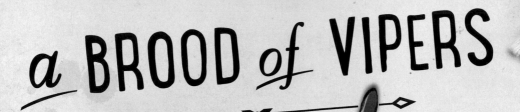

a BROOD of VIPERS

The Plantagenets were not a peaceful family, and took sibling squabbles to a new level! They were ambitious, ruthless and often went to war with each other. Henry II called his children 'a brood of vipers' (a type of venomous snake) as they were so vicious and untrustworthy. For their part the sons couldn't wait to get their hands on Henry's empire as quickly as they could.

Henry's sons wanted more control of the empire than Henry would allow them to have. Encouraged by their mother, Eleanor of Aquitaine, John's eldest brothers fought against their father from 1173–1174 to try to seize the empire. Eventually, a peace treaty was reached and Eleanor was imprisoned; but it was only a matter of time before war would break out again. There were further outbreaks of fighting in 1183 between Richard and his brother Henry (until Henry died from an illness called dysentery) and in 1184 when Richard and John squabbled over territory.

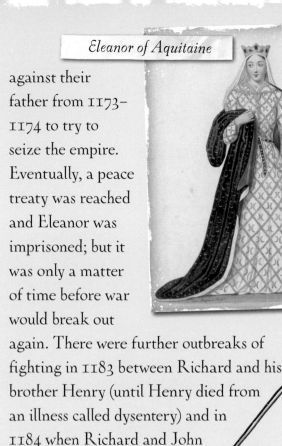

WHO WAS SHE?

John's mother, Eleanor of Aquitaine (born around 1122 – died 1204), was one of the most influential women of the Middle Ages. She married two kings (before Henry she had been married to King Louis VII of France) and was mother to two more (Richard and John). Heavily involved in the politics of the Angevin empire she remained in control of her homeland of Aquitaine until her death.

In order to give John some land Henry II made him Lord of Ireland. Henry had invaded Ireland in 1171 and decided that now John was 17 years old, he should be responsible for governing the country. John travelled there in 1184 but quickly managed to turn the Irish chieftains against him by publicly mocking them. They rebelled against him and John returned to England in disgrace.

WELL I NEVER!

During the Middle Ages knights practised their skills in sports including tournaments in which they charged at each other on horseback in mock battles. It was highly dangerous and in 1186 John's brother Geoffrey died in such a pretend battle.

THE LIONHEART

In 1189, Richard decided to take his inheritance early and by force. Joining with King Philip II of France, he went to war against his father. John sided with his father to begin with, but seeing that Richard was winning, changed sides! On the 6 July 1189, Henry, distraught by the news his youngest son had turned against him too, died in the city of Chinon in France. Richard was now King.

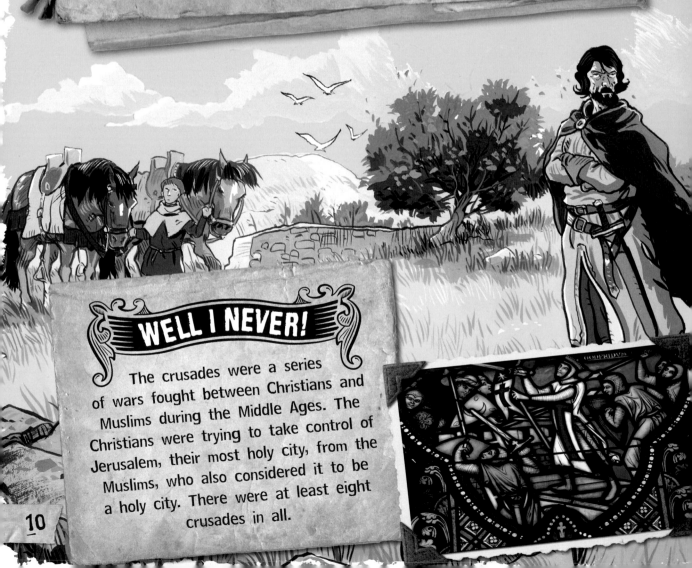

WELL I NEVER!

The crusades were a series of wars fought between Christians and Muslims during the Middle Ages. The Christians were trying to take control of Jerusalem, their most holy city, from the Muslims, who also considered it to be a holy city. There were at least eight crusades in all.

Many myths have been passed down through time about the two brothers. People say Richard was taller and broader than John; but no evidence has been found for this.

Richard was a fearless leader and was nicknamed 'the Lionheart'. In contrast, all John seemed to inspire was mistrust. When Richard named his nephew Arthur as his heir, the king knew he would have to work hard to keep his brother as a supporter and not an enemy.

Before his coronation Richard had promised to join the crusades – a holy war to return Jerusalem to Christian control. Richard was worried that John would attempt to overthrow him while he was away. To buy John's loyalty, Richard gave him large amounts of land in England and married him to the wealthy Isabella of Gloucester. In return John had to promise not enter England but to stay in France for three years by which time Richard should have returned. John agreed to the terms, but in reality was waiting for an opportunity to seize power himself.

WHO WAS HE?

Richard the Lionheart (1157–1199)

Richard has the reputation of being an English hero but in reality he spent less than six months in the country. He had all the attributes of a good knight: he was an excellent fighter, well-mannered and a lover of music and poetry. However, he could also be incredibly cruel and was guilty of terrible war crimes, such as massacring thousands of prisoners in cold blood.

TREACHERY

Although John had been forbidden to return to England that's exactly what he did. Richard had left trusted nobles in charge of the country, but John set himself up as an alternative leader. Then in 1192, events took a sudden turn in John's favour – Richard was taken prisoner on his way back from the crusades!

Poor weather had forced Richard to travel overland, where he was imprisoned by Duke Leopold of Austria and in 1194 handed over to the German Emperor Henry IV. During the Middle Ages it was common for important prisoners to be ransomed – held prisoner until an amount of money was paid. The emperor put Richard up for ransom of 100,000 marks – an absolute fortune at the time. On top of this Richard would have to supply 50 ships and 200 knights to serve the emperor for a year! This was too good an opportunity for John to pass up. He made a pact with King Philip and made his bid to take Richard's crown.

★ The ★ legend of Robin Hood

One of the most well-known opponents of John's attempt to rule was Robin Hood. Famous for robbing from the rich and giving to the poor, actual proof of Robin's existence is hard to come by. He may have lived in Nottingham, or Yorkshire, or Staffordshire – or may not have existed at all.

What John had not counted on was the level of resistance he would face – particularly from his own mother. Eleanor of Aquitaine helped organise the fight against John's attempt to become King. She managed to raise the ransom as barons loyal to Richard fought John's troops. Eleanor's efforts were not in vain; Richard was set free and returned to England.

WELL I NEVER!

When important nobles, such as Richard, were captured they were often held to ransom rather than killed. Captives lived decent lives; they had access to good food and were treated with respect. After all, they were worth a lot of money and needed to be looked after.

KING JOHN!

When John heard that Richard was returning to England he fled to France, but Richard came looking for him. However there was a surprising turn of events; Richard forgave John for his attempt to seize the throne. Why is unclear – it may have been that Richard did not want to cause problems with John's supporters. Even so, no one could have predicted what would happen next.

While Richard was away fighting to secure his empire he was mortally wounded whilst holding a castle to siege. It may be that on his deathbed Richard changed his earlier decision to pass the throne to his nephew, and named John as the next king - but no one knows for sure. When Richard died on the 6 April 1199, John seized the throne against the claims of his nephew Arthur.

Not everybody accepted the new king. Many people still supported the claim to the throne made by Arthur, particularly in northern France where Arthur lived. Almost inevitably war broke out again; this time in France.

Troublesome ★ neighbours ★

When William the Conqueror, a Norman duke, took over England in 1066 his battles against the French king became England's concern, too. This is why England and France were often at war from this point onwards.

IN OTHER NEWS

NEW NUMBERS

The Middle Ages saw great advances in learning in Europe. In mathematics Roman numerals were still used, but during the 1100s the Arabic numerals that we use today began to gain favour. The big advantage that Arabic numerals had was that they had a number for zero, which Roman numerals didn't. This made them much easier to use than Roman numerals.

$$1 = I$$
$$2 = II$$
$$3 = III$$
$$4 = IV$$
$$5 = V$$
$$6 = VI$$
$$7 = VII$$
$$8 = VIII$$
$$9 = IX$$
$$10 = X$$
$$50 = L$$
$$100 = C$$
$$500 = D$$
$$1000 = M$$

a ROYAL LIFE

Life during the Middle Ages was tough. Most people lived in the countryside and worked the land. Without machines to do heavy or monotonous work, it was a hard and tiring life. This did not apply to the nobility who did not do manual work. John was the highest ranking noble, so his life should have been the easiest of all.

To a certain extent it was. While most people lived in crude huts made of wood and mud, John lived in castles made of stone. While all women wore long tunics and men wore shorter tunics made of wool, the quality of these garments was different for peasants and nobility. John would have worn fine linens and even silk imported from the east.

However, it wasn't always easy to be king. John lived in almost constant fear for his life – there were many men who looked at his throne with envious eyes. John lived in castles for protection from enemies, not just to shelter from the rain and cold.

This scene shows a king dining. Historians think it may be Henry II.

John was also careful not to stay in one place for too long in case armies formed against him in other parts of the kingdom. Rebellions might occur anywhere in his kingdom so John would travel to quell them. This meant lots of travel, which meant riding on horseback over rough roads in all weathers – an uncomfortable life for a king.

★ Food ★ for thought

Although the nobility enjoyed a more varied and plentiful diet than peasants it wasn't necessarily healthier. The biggest problem with the food the nobility ate was the lack of vegetables as vegetables were considered peasant food.

TRUE or FALSE?

KING HENRY I, JOHN'S GRANDFATHER, DIED AFTER EATING TOO MANY LAMPREYS.

false Although it's true that Henry did die after eating lampreys (an eel-like fish), the idea that it was because he had eaten too many only appeared hundreds of years after his death. However, lampreys can be toxic if not cleaned properly so Henry may have died of food poisoning.

PEACE and MARRIAGE

The war in France was only a few months old and John had already just avoided being captured. John knew to his cost that war was expensive and often achieved little, so should be avoided if at all possible. Instead of fighting on he made a truce with Arthur, but this peace came at a heavy price. Arthur was under the protection of the French king, Philip, so John was forced to accept Philip as his overlord.

This meant that John could keep what was left of his French lands, but had to acknowledge that Philip was the greater of the two kings and rightfully owned John's French lands. John's unwillingness to fight and the ease with which he gave up control of his lands earned him the nickname 'Softsword'. In the eyes of the people the difference with his brother Richard could not have been greater.

John was seen as weak and untrustworthy, but his reputation was doomed to sink even lower.

IN OTHER NEWS

THE FOURTH CRUSADE

Pope Innocent declared a crusade to liberate the holy city of Jerusalem from the Muslims. This was the fourth crusade and would last from 1202 to 1204. However the crusade would never make it as far as Jerusalem. Short of cash, the crusaders ended up raiding the cities of Zara and Constantinople instead as a way of raising money, before eventually drifting back home.

In 1199 John had his first marriage annulled, or ended, and married Isabella of Angoulême instead. Isabella owned land in areas that would strengthen John's empire, but unfortunately Isabella was already engaged to an important French noble called Hugh de Lusignan. Rebellion broke out in the Lusignan lands and John found himself at war again.

TRUE or FALSE?

MEDIEVAL MAPS OF THE WORLD PUT JERUSALEM AT THEIR CENTRE.

true Jerusalem was the most holy city for Christians and was therefore the most important place in the world. So, on medieval maps, Jerusalem always appeared at the very centre.

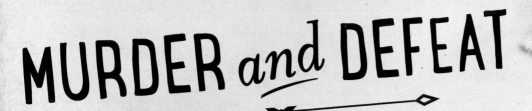

MURDER and DEFEAT

John managed to suppress the rebellions in the Lusignan territories but the war took a turn for the worse. King Philip of France declared that John's behaviour had broken the terms of their truce. Philip proclaimed Arthur to be the rightful king of John's French lands and the two of them launched a two-pronged attack on John's forces.

Young Arthur was imprisoned in Rouen Castle.

Although the war started badly for John it took a decisive swing in his favour when he managed to surprise Arthur's forces and capture his young rival. It was a tactical masterstroke. Not only had John defeated one enemy, but Philip was forced to divide his own army to try and come to Arthur's aid.

However, shortly after being taken prisoner, Arthur disappeared. It was rumoured that he had been killed by King John. Whether this was true or not, it was true that other rebel leaders had also perished in John's prisons. Meanwhile John was alienating his former allies – at precisely the time when conflicts and uprisings were springing up all over John's empire. John was faced with a war that was too expensive to win. By 1204 he had lost most of his French lands – it was a disaster.

★ Rough ★ justice

Law and order in the Middle Ages was often unfair and cruel. Before 1215 there was no trial by jury and common punishments included blinding and having hands chopped off for crimes such as theft.

IN OTHER NEWS

A FUTURE CAPITAL

In 1204 people began building a village near the dam on the Amstel River and Amsterdam was born. The city would become the capital city of the Netherlands, itself one of England's chief rivals for territory and trade.

TROUBLE at HOME

Things had been going badly for John in France but if he was hoping for an easier time in England he was going to be disappointed. John needed to assert his authority, but in a few short years he managed to fall out with some of his most trusted allies and possibly the most important man in Europe at the time, Pope Innocent III.

Trouble began with the death of the Archbishop of Canterbury, the head of the Church in England. John wanted to appoint his friend, John de Grey, to be the new archbishop, but the Pope appointed a cardinal called Stephen Langton instead. John refused to accept Langton, banned him from the country and seized Church property. The Pope responded by excommunicating England. In the Middle Ages this was as serious as it got. On a personal level people believed it meant you would never go to heaven. On a political level it meant that you were more likely to be invaded as the Pope would not come to your aid if asked.

John was also worried about the power his own barons held. Almost on a whim he fell out with some of his oldest friends, stripping them of their property and land. He even imprisoned the wife and child of one – William de Braose – and left them to starve to death. John was making more enemies than he could cope with.

Stephen Langton

TRUE or FALSE?

JOHN WAS THE FIRST KING OF ENGLAND WHO COULD SPEAK ENGLISH.

false All kings from the time of William the Conqueror spoke only French. John, like his father Henry II, spoke French, but probably understood at least a few words in English.

William the Conqueror

from BAD to WORSE

By 1212 simmering discontent had turned into open rebellion in Wales. John crushed the uprising and in the process improved his reputation as a military commander. However he was aware that he was surrounded by enemies and that couldn't continue. It was time to make peace with the Pope.

Peace came with heavy terms. John was forced to hand England over to Pope Innocent III as a fiefdom – John was still king, but England became part of the Church's empire. In addition John had to pay a large annual rent to the Pope, and make compensation to those churchmen whose property he had seized. Finally, John also had to accept Stephen Langton as Archbishop of Canterbury. It was a humiliating climb down but in John's view a necessary one.

John then decided that this was a good time to retake his French lands by force. Although his campaign started well, it ended disastrously with him losing more land to King Philip in decisive military defeats.

John returned to England having spent all his money on the war and with his reputation, once again, in tatters.

If John was dreaming of yet another expedition to France then he soon realised he had more pressing concerns. Many of his barons had lost faith in him – and in 1215 a full-scale rebellion broke out in England. The rebel army, led by Robert FitzWalter, captured London. John's situation had gone from bad to worse.

★ Home security ★

Castles were more than fancy homes for nobility; they were a statement of power and wealth. A well-positioned castle dominated the landscape and from there all the nearby roads and rivers could be brought under the castle-owner's control.

MAGNA CARTA

Although John had lost the support of a large number of his barons, he still had the support of the Pope and was still the king. The barons were also in the odd position of having a rebellion without a clear idea of who they wanted to take over. The situation had to be resolved. A meeting was arranged between the two sides at Runnymede near Windsor.

The barons presented John with a document setting out their demands. It was based, they claimed, on the coronation charter that Henry I had issued in which promises were made to look after the interests of the king's subjects. In effect the document sought to control the amount of power the king could exert over a range of different issues, such as justice, trade and money that was payable to the king. Many of the ideas were revolutionary: no imprisonment without trial; everyone had the right to access to a court of law; and that the Church had powers independent of the King. The document was named Magna Carta or the Great Charter.

IN OTHER NEWS

GENGHIS KHAN INVADES CHINA

In around 1214 Mongol leader Genghis Khan attacked and took control of the city Zhongdu (now the Chinese capital Beijing). Born around 1167, Genghis managed to unite Mongol tribes under his leadership, and created an empire that stretched over much of Asia.

Signing Magna Carter was a massive humiliation for John as his barons were telling him, the king, what he could and could not do. However John was short of other options. The document was signed with his seal and copies made and distributed throughout the country.

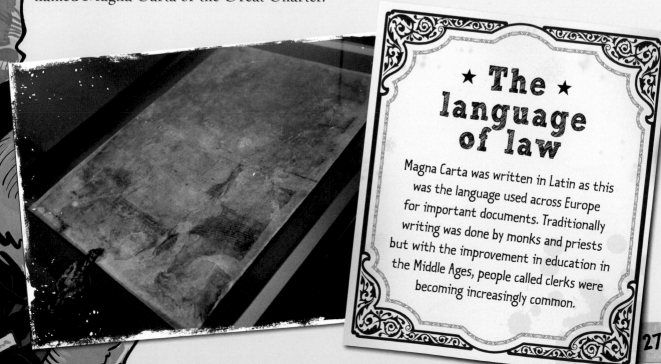

★ The ★ language of law

Magna Carta was written in Latin as this was the language used across Europe for important documents. Traditionally writing was done by monks and priests but with the improvement in education in the Middle Ages, people called clerks were becoming increasingly common.

THE END

John was not going to bear the humiliation of Magna Carta for long. Almost immediately he renounced the document and sought the support of the Pope for his actions. The barons rose up again, but John scored decisive victories against the rebels. The tide seemed to be turning in John's favour; but there was bad news to come.

The rebels decided that Louis, the son of King Philip II of France should be their new ruler. An invasion fleet from France landed and quickly gained control of London and much of southern England. The tide had turned again.

To make matters worse John's health was failing him as well as his luck. In Lincolnshire his army baggage train got stuck in the boggy land around the River Welland and was sucked beneath the mud. Not only did John lose his

household goods, but his treasure too and – according to some accounts – the crown jewels. Days later John died of dysentery in Newark, Nottinghamshire.

The rebels decided a young English prince was preferable to a French king and declared John's son Henry to be king – even though Henry was only nine at the time! Louis and his French troops were driven from the country and peace, of a sort, returned.

King John's body was taken to Worcester to be buried. His tomb still stands in Worcester Cathedral today.

★ John today ★

John has a terrible reputation, but was he really that bad? Certainly he was cruel, but so were other rulers at the time. However, unlike many kings John took a keen interest in the law and would listen to court cases wherever he was in the country – whether they involved nobles or peasants. Perhaps his reputation suffered because he fell out with the Church and most histories were written by monks and priests. Or perhaps he was just too deceitful and too harsh for his own good and for the good of the country?

TIMELINE

1154	Henry II, John's father, becomes king
1156	William, John's oldest brother, dies at two years of age
1167	birth of John
	birth of Temujin, later to be known as Genghis Khan, leader of the Mongol Empire
1175	end of the Toltec Empire which controlled what is now modern-day Mexico
1180	Louis VII of France dies
	Philip II Augustus becomes the new French king
1181	Henry and Richard revolt against their father, Henry II
1183	Henry, John's brother, dies of dysentery
1184	John and Richard fight over territory in France
	John is sent to Ireland and returns in disgrace
1186	Geoffrey, John's brother, dies at a tournament
1189	start of the Third Crusade
	Henry II, John's father, dies
	Richard the Lionheart becomes king
1192	Richard is taken prisoner and held for ransom
1199	Richard dies from crossbow injuries
	John becomes king
	Joan, John's sister, dies in childbirth
1200	John's first marriage is annulled and he marries Isabella of Angoulême
1203	Arthur, John's nephew and rival to his throne, dies in John's prison
1204	Eleanor of Aquitaine, John's mother, dies
1209	John and England excommunicated by the Pope
1212	rebellion breaks out in Wales
1214	Eleanor, John's sister, dies
1215	rebellion breaks out in England
	signing of Magna Carta
1216	John dies

GLOSSARY

baggage train the carts that carried an army's supplies and equipment

barons nobles; often referred to as 'lords'

bloated swollen or fat

brood a group of (or in a different context it can mean to think over things)

cardinal an important member of the Church

Christians people who follow the teachings of Jesus

coronation the ceremony where a king or queen is crowned

crown jewels the crowns and other valuables a king or queen uses on formal occasions

deceitful lying and untrustworthy

descendent a direct relative of a person born earlier than them

envious jealous

inheritance when a person dies and leaves money, property or titles to someone

lances long, spear-like weapons often used by men on horseback

liberate free

mortally wounded an injury that will kill the victim

Muslims people who follow the teachings of the prophet Mohammed

peasants people who worked the land. They were the least powerful members of society.

politics the organisation and running of a government or kingdom

rebellion when people try to get rid of their ruler or leader by force

renounced when a person spoke out against something they had supported

seal the king's sign made in melted wax

siblings brothers and sisters

squabbled argued over

tunic a long, loose item of clothing

tyrant a cruel and unjust ruler

further information

BOOKS

Barmy Biogs: Crackpot Kings, Queens and other Daft Royals by Kay Barnham (Wayland, 2013)

Kings and Queens by Tony Robinson (Red Fox, 2014)

The Gruesome Truth About: The Middle Ages by Matt Buckingham (Wayland, 2012)

The Magna Carta: Cornerstone of the Constitution by Roberta Baxter (Heinemann Educational Books, 2012)

Who's who in British History by Bob Fowke (Wayland, 2014)

WEBSITES

www.bbc.co.uk/schools/primaryhistory/british_history/magna_carta/

www.theschoolrun.com/homework-help/the-magna-carta

www.historylearningsite.co.uk/magna_carta.htm

PLACES TO VISIT

The Magna Carta Memorial is at Runnymede, Windsor Road, Old Windsor, Surrey SL4 2JL
The four original copies of Magna Carta are kept at:

* The British Library (two copies), 96 Euston Road, London NW1 2DP
* Salisbury Cathedral, 6 The Close, Salisbury, Wilts SP1 2EJ
* Lincoln Cathedral, Minster Yard, Lincoln LN2 1PX

King John's tomb is at Worcester Cathedral, 8 College Yard, Worcester WR1 2LA

INDEX

More history titles available
from Wayland...

Best and Worst Jobs in...

978 0 7502 8736 4

978 0 7502 8740 1

Truth or Busted

978 0 7502 8129 4

978 0 7502 8130 0

What they don't tell you about...

978 0 7502 8167 6

978 0 7502 8047 1

Awfully Ancient

978 0 7502 7991 8

978 0 7502 7987 1

EPIC

978 0 7502 8761 6

978 0 7502 8755 5

Explore!

978 0 7502 8860 6

978 0 7502 9549 9

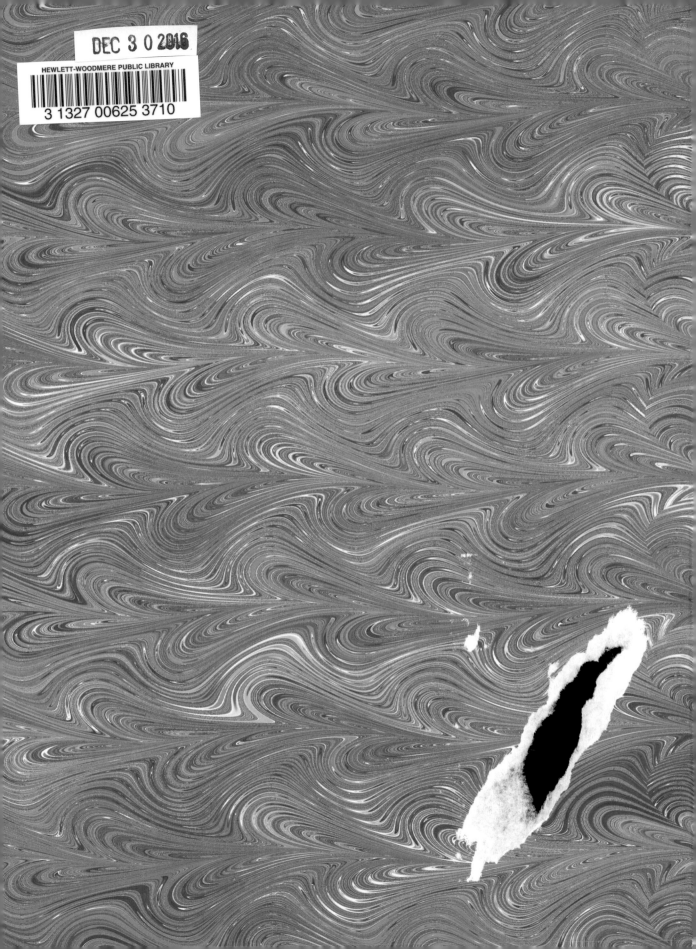